The Love S

MW01577451

Why you are already in my heart, as for me, there is no reason which to avoid the wind. Only we could be like that, verily only we would like to be.

For it is for us to hold, for the sweetheart in you, who looks at me, It is at that one time, I would start sinking, ardently, just there is none to be,

To go quickly towards the evening sun, it is time for us to encounter, we too, will repeat many times this journey, the love story of many dreams. Either one of us fell to love, that is to say, that we found a world before the wind. Where there is a promise it is for us to hold.

I try remembering the next time we'll be together, and I find I am not just an image that can be seen, but the spirit that is hidden within you, deep inside of you.

I tried remembering the next time we would meet, and yes our words remained, we should have loved, we should have lived. Why you are already in my heart! As for me, there was a reason which to be the wind, and only we could be like that.

Soul mates second coming of the sun, when will you believe, I want to build a garden, upon the waters, for us to walk upon.

Why there could be more for us, but is that truly our dreams, that it will be, Is it too much to call it love, so we will never have to say good bye,

Please don't just walk away, and know our love is here to stay, Soul mates of the gardens, when will you believe the second coming of the sun and the love story of many dreams.

Carolyn Joyce Carty American Poet

8336756R0

Made in the USA
Charleston, SC
29 May 2011